APR 2013

SHORTLY THEREAFTER

poetry by

Colin D. Halloran

WINNER OF THE 2012 MAIN STREET RAG POETRY BOOK AWARD

MAIN STREET RAG PUBLISHING COMPANY
CHARLOTTE, NORTH CAROLINA

Acknowledgements:

The New York Times: "Monuments"
Caper Literary Journal: "Carnivale, Tarin Kowt"
Long River Run: "Vigil"
San Pedro River Review: "Raining in Germany," "I'm Reminded More in
    Winter," "Anomalies in Vapid Landscape"
phati'tude: Bridging the Cultural Divide: Remembering September 11th:
    "Echoes," "Democracy, Tea, and Belly Dancers"
Stone Canoe: "Lines Composed (A Few Miles Above Kandahar)"
BluePrint Review: "The Moon's Still Up," "I Want to Paint the Sunrise,"
    "Tightroping Trucks"
Workers Write! Tales from the Combat Zone: "QRF"
The Spotlight: "Contradictions"

Library of Congress Control Number: 2012944337

ISBN: 978-1-59948-383-2

Produced in the United States of America

Mint Hill Books
PO Box 690100
Charlotte, NC 28227
www.MainStreetRag.com

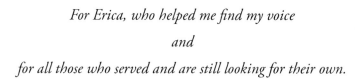

For Erica, who helped me find my voice
and
for all those who served and are still looking for their own.

CONTENTS

III.

IV.

I

FOXTROT

I got in a month of college before my orders came,
but I wouldn't just end the semester. Not me.
I worked double, prepping for mobilization,
being a college freshman, only four courses.

Mobilization: getting equipment, medical evaluations,
paperwork, paperwork, paperwork, training for combat,
formations, movements, how to stop a sucking chest wound.

College: the history of theatre, anthro: "diversity and inequality",
Mann and Hesse: "the artist in society", women and American law.

Textbooks, novels, plays, court cases, essays.

Field manuals, intro to Pashto, facts about Afghanistan
and a different writing assignment: my last will and testament.

At 19 what do you have to leave to those you love?
A 4 year-old Jetta, stereo, CD collection.
I leave my concert t-shirts to…
Harder than any essay I could've been assigned.

And I had to miss class, not too much, but enough,
apparently, to violate attendance policies,
get me an F in Anthro – though my work produced an A.

I had the documentation,
the prof knew the situation,
but I guess I went against his politics.

So I went to war with an F in anthropology
and a form written will,

leaving what little I had in the hands of my brother,
and forcing me to spend what little downtime I could muster
between missions on global phone calls to university officials
so if I returned from the desert, rendered my will unnecessary,
there wouldn't be a black mark on my transcript.

FOOTLOCKER

Each soldier is issued a footlocker—
approx. 32 ½ x 15 ¾ x 13 ¾ "—
for personal effects:
clothes, magazines, movies, mementos
of a home they're leaving behind,
or essentials like cigarettes and jerky.

Pornography and booze have no place
in these silver-latched intimate havens,
they violate General Order 1.

Each person's is different, though
there are some items found across the board,
namely baby wipes and sunscreen,
but they say you can learn a lot about a man
from his box's contents.

My box is my own.
A five pound jar of Skippy,
the latest issues of *Surfing* and *Whitewater*—
so at least my dreams are not left dry in the desert—
most of the remaining space is dedicated to an infantryman's anomaly: books.
I can't seem to go to war without Shakespeare, Uris, Whitman, Keats.
I am not a typical grunt
is what my footlocker says.

SHOTS

Shots.
Smallpox. Hep. A. B.

Shots.
Boarding. Arriving.
Carolina. Kyrgyzstan.
Bragg. Bagram.

Shots.
Fired. Received. Returned.

Shots.
Echo. Remembered.

Shots.
Whiskey. Straight.
Poured. Drunk.

Shots.
Forgotten.

Never.

CONTRADICTIONS

Snowcapped peaks watch over
lush, fertile valleys that cling desperately
to shrinking riverbanks.

The harsh freeze of the mountain winter disputes
the singeing heat of the mid-July desert.

Pop shots and car bombs
seldom scattered amidst
tea, handshakes, embraces.

Gap-toothed smiles of school children
reflected in the tired eyes
of creased faces worn by war.

SIXTH TOUR

The first tour, he was one of us:
fully treaded boots,
no sand or sweat stained uniform,
fresh faced for that short stay abroad,
6 months to Kuwaiti liberation.

Then, with a wife to leave behind,
to Bosnia to bear a few months' witness
before a trip to Central America
in new capacity, making the move
from frontline to hangars,
hands on Blackhawks, not rifles.

The time between two stints in Iraq
brought a beautiful baby girl,
so on the second he could learn
how to leave behind a wife *and* child.

Then two weeks before we left
for his return to frontline combat,
a baby boy, one more reason
for the rest of us to fight for his survival.

And after the first attack and the command's debriefing,
it was he who went from room to room, making sure
that we, his guys, were managing. Ok. Processing
the shit we'd all just seen.

THE THEATRE OF WAR

Opening night jitters.

We stage our perimeter, strategically blocked
so backs are never turned: maximize the space.

No more "what do you do in the real world?"
We know what our roles are now.

Lights go down.

Fires dot the expanse we face. Spectators? Viewers?
Or will they be the unscripted addition to this scene—
compact compound, our set, walls higher in the west,
we line the eastward trench behind dirt mounds
that serve as walls, Dutch sniper on the central roof
standing two stories above perimeter buildings—

Testing our improvisation, pushing our limits,
forcing us to slip out of character and forget
who we've become?

THE VELCRO NOW SUGGESTS IMPERMANENCE

or a willingness to change
rotate out
or simply disappear.

Closest to the heart reads *US Army*
in print as bold as the other
and just as removable
as though country and service were socks
changed daily to match your mood.

Or is the Velcro, with its hooks and eyes,
metaphor
the way it latches on to what's already there
offering more points of contact
than thread and needle would allow?

Across the chest the name tape
indicates what it will, and I have two:
one with my last name,
(in the Army you just don't do firsts)
the other reads *Frylock*,
cartoon mastermind of Hungerforce fame.

And which of these two names—
one paternal, the other false—
and a designation I share
with those around me
says more?

SILENT NIGHT

Uruzgan Province, Afghanistan: May 2006

The air is warm, still.

In the harsh light of the sun, the landscape loses its features,
washed out into monotonous russets.

But by the soft light of the moon, the mountains play in blues,
hitting deep indigo riffs off smooth cobalt crescendos.

Though the sun escaped behind these distant peaks,
the darkness is not absolute.

The lights of a multitude of stars kiss the ground:
a snapshot of serenity.
A moment of peace in this turbulent world I've been living in.
Trying to live.
A scene unobtainable in the ambient-lit nights of home.

Home.
The word sounds foreign softly spoken in this alien landscape.

Unholy.

A distant sound breaks
through the silence of the warm desert night,
the stillness penetrated by more
than the piercing light of long-passed stars.

The silence was illusion.
Serenity existed in isolation.
Stillness: a distant memory.

I am stirred to action, snapped from that seeming dreamscape back into the death-laden landscape that once existed only in the worst of dreams.

Beating blades bearing bodies move slowly closer.

All we do: wait.

DEATH, LIKE AN UNCLE

I have no recollection of
his face before age five, then
brief visits from time-to-time, just enough
to make sure he was not forgotten.

But death in New England's small towns is not
the same as in Uruzgan's blood-soaked sands.

At home, it was always neat, clean, put in
a varnished box and neatly tied up: the half-Windsor
at the base of my father's stiff neck—just a boy then;
many would consider me to be so still.

Transplanted, death now seems unfamiliar.
Hanging untamed on the breath of martyrs,

it is not efficiently contained in the rows of morgues,
it scatters itself haphazardly within the blast
radius; uncontained by mortal grids, lacking apparent
logic, and lingering, following our every move.

BOY FOR SALE

Fourteen, eleven, twenty.

The taller boy
approaches across the barren land
with a piece of paper in his hand,

a picture of the second.
Eleven years old, he hears
the asking price for his own life.

Twenty dollars: negotiable.

The place has come to this:
boys asking you
to buy their brothers.

FIELD HOSPITAL

It is not the chronically ill who pass through these doors.
The beds are not filled with the old and infirm.

In them lie the ruined bodies of youth,
their faces so recently lit by the desire for
candy
pens
clean water
soccer balls
a new team to play against.

In this room,
stark sterility contradicts the desert's dust up,
IVs replace crayons
breathing tubes, candy
death, desire.

QUARTERS

Aboveground basement,
that's what it seems to be;
the only source of natural light:
a two-pane slat kept high above our heads.

At night we cut the darkness with a solitary bulb,
bare-faced and buzzing,
silence disallowed.

The single desk—or maybe it's a table—
lends a monastic air to cut the prison cell sense
created by whitewashed concrete walls
and at least one occupant too many.

There's an air freshener—
battery run, automatic, badly needed—
up in the corner by the slat.
Its hiss, emitted day and night,
just loud enough to wake
whoever's fortunate enough
to have the time to sleep.

ANOMALIES IN VAPID LANDSCAPE

It offered us the nomadic camp,
tawny and masked at first, with its camels
and dust-blasted blankets for shelter,
but brimming with vibrant colors and characters
on closer approach.

Their faces as ranging as the landscape
they made themselves a part of—craggy and creviced—
smiling through linguistic barriers that even
stood between them and their countrymen,
they accepted our gifts of food and drink,
and shook our hands with vigor.

Here, hours later, another break:
poppies, white and pink poking out
from lush greens huddled around
the only trace of water for miles.

And as opiatic pastels
emerge from green and tan,
darker figures fleck the fertile expanse.
Binoculars reveal AK-47s in hand
as half a dozen men patrol the fields
whose crop will feed their village.

SANDSTORM

The sand kicks up, swirling like Turner's brushstrokes.

In this violent dance all is lost,
buried, blinded, if only for a moment.

When this two-minute miracle ends,
a palpable calm permeates
the witness, leaving him to wonder
Was it all just a dream,
or is this tranquility: settled dust and stillness?

MR. SHINGLES

They call me names.

Not like those kids in the back of the bus.
(Man, how time flies…)

These are different:

Advent Calendar.
The Christmas Tree.
(TCT in an acronym happy world)
And my favorite: they call me Mr. Shingles.

Pouches. Tan on grey.
One short of a dozen.
Strapped to the front of my vest.

No chocolates to be found inside.

0.23 kg—that's roughly half a pound—
H-E—that's High Explosive—
Rounds—grenades.

The joys of being grenadier.
Six extra pounds of volatility.

5 meter kill radius. 15m CR[1].
These are the things you need to know.
Knowledge to be effective in the field.
Knowledge that one round to the chest
(a chest maybe 70% covered)
will take out you and anyone unfortunate enough
to be in that CR.

Boom.

So they call me Mr. Shingles.
And we laugh. I laugh.

Because what else can you do
when you are set to blow.

ECHOES

The call to prayer:
a five times daily reminder
of where I am, what I've become,
ripping me from the scenes I see now
only in rough-hewn, oft-interrupted dreams:

birch flecked island perched on the edge of a northern lake, deceptively calm,
fed by rivers whose rage increases as they work their way down mountains.

The call to prayer:
launched from shaky speakers
on each mosque's pinnacle, a call
to strange echoes of New England
summers I've swapped for sand and blood,
increasing turmoil meets contingent calm:

the edges, where that island stood sentinel, still, composed, spreading each river's
head-long tumble wide, where someone once told me that God is in the sunrise.

The call to prayer:
an attempt at applied symmetry
ordering disorder,
even spreading of a river's rush,
a lake, serene:

at its center, out from under Katahdin's shadow, where the surface showed moun-
tain and sky inverted, the wind spoke tumult, threatening just off God's reflection.

The call to prayer:
a return to this false serenity, scenes of peace
masking unknown dangers as we are forced
to stop, delay the mission, so our local counterparts can pray
in shifts:

that island was our shelter, as we huddled, windbound and waiting,
for calm or chaos to engulf us as we crossed at sunrise.

The call to prayer:
for us, a cigarette break,
as we watch for God's reflection
and the violence that awaits us
just above the surface.

II

SPRING OFFENSIVE

Sadness is a white bird that does not come near a battlefield.
Soldiers commit a sin when they feel sad.
—*A Soldier Dreams of White Tulips*, Mahmoud Darwish

I. I HAVE HEARD THE MULLAH SPEAK

That we have fathers
and they have fathers
and so we all are sons.

That we have sons
and they have sons
and so we all are fathers.

Their fathers make us sons
our sons make them fathers
and so we all are brothers.

But Cain buried Abel
and we are our fathers.

Allahuakbar

Just a boy when the Russians
left this barren desert somehow
more scorched than when they came,

it was days, maybe weeks before news
wound its way from Kabul to the south.
We rejoiced. I did not know why.

My father rejoiced. And I rejoiced in his
rejoicing. We become our fathers.

Allahuakbar

Our fathers become our sons.
I have a father, and a son whose
son I will become.

Allahuakbar

Fourteen mortars. some as old as I,
packed and wired in this truck that
last week brought melons to market.

My father was a farmer, forced
to take up arms to save his sons.
And we become our fathers.

Allahuakbar

I followed all instructions:
the wiring, the waiting.
I wait. And think of my son.

Allahuakbar

The first truck passes: my sign.
I think of my son, and pull the old
pick-up from behind the hut.

Allahuakbar

It is the moment that will save my son,
that will ensure the comfort of my father,
that I must become Kabil, and bury my brother.

Allahuakbar

I see past the barrel to his eyes:
he is my father's son. Yet too young to be a father.
My brother—resolute.

Allahuakbar

Sweaty palms fumble for the trigger.
I am a farmer, but we become our fathers.

Allahuakbar

I look in my brother's eyes
as my son's name crosses my lips…

Allahuakbar

II. REFLECTIONS

The entire mirror is black
as if the sky has fallen in on itself.
At the center, the flicker of flame:
a glimpse.

Absent: the cinematic pillar:
smoke gently drifting to the heavens.

That's it.
Everything changed.

I think I felt the earth shake.
I think I heard shouts.

They say the training takes over.
It does.

I count the Hummers
in the blackened mirror.

No time to wonder.
It happened.

A haze casts itself
over the ensuing hour.

A two-second assessment:
scan for danger-close.
Engage the brakes.

Out of the truck.
Perimeter.
Someone's shouting my name,
telling me to push out.

I'm already there.

They say the training takes over...

I risk a half-glance back.

The black wall—gone,
little more than a wisp.

Flames cling to the remnants
of some twisted metal beast.
Maybe a pickup, maybe one of ours.

Nearby: a smoldering heap
that will later reveal itself
to be a body:
Charred. Limbless.

A scan of turrets: Big D's down.
No time to think about him:
Have to hold the perimeter.

They say the training takes over.
It does. It did.

In mere seconds it's taken in,
then pushed aside.

Images stored to
reflect on later that night
as I lie in bed
wondering what it was that
cracked the Gates of Hell.

MORNING COMMUTE

That's the spot he ran to.
Where he came to say hello: a wave and a salute.

I drive by it every day.

I sped down this road,
escorting bodies back to the hospital.
broken youth, behind burned uniform.

Bloodied soldier tight-roping consciousness,
then the boy: arteries so cleanly cut
as shrapnel raced from ground to chest.

A call for candy, a classic case
wrong time, wrong place.

They cracked his chest,
the surgeon tenderly caressing the tiny heart,
gently coercing it back to life:
soft palpitations to return color left to the sand.

It beats on its own.

The lungs are a different story.
For two days machines insist on life.

A coloring book, a doll:
a smile.

Hope.

The lungs follow the heart,
filling on their own free will.

One day.

Then he falters.

Machines are reattached.
The smile in his eyes
begins to fade.

That's the spot.
I drive by it every day.

IT'S 3 A.M.

Or maybe 4, or 2.

It doesn't matter.

The staggered breaths and stifled sobs are hourly tolls throughout these nights.
You can't help but relive it. Can't help but see him, I'm sure.

But I can't know for sure what it is you see, or what it was you saw.
For me it was all just sound and blackness. The blackness that engulfed you,
that raked Russian metal through your skin, singed the smile from your face...

And now back here, in this cement cube we share, I rise to rock you back
to sleep, hands and head engulfed in bandages as you had been engulfed
in flames, and you, bear of a man, sobbing into my shoulder.

DEMOCRACY, TEA, AND BELLYDANCERS

Just another sunny day in Afghanistan,
(rain can't find its way)
a mission to the governor's palace,
(small suburban home by the standards I grew up with)
and today, once my truck's inside the gates, I join his palace guards.

They offer me weak tea
(it's rude to decline)
and we sit there sipping
(leaves steeped in water: the new universal language).

It's a quiet day in town
(even extremists don't like working when it's 120°)
and there's a laid back air among us.

One guard reads a newspaper
(the rest of us sip and smile),
and as he gets to the back page,
I realize the paper's not from around here
(the South is still strict on women).

A grin spreads across his face
and when he's finished turning
the page—it features two women,
bellies and ankles exposed—to face me,
his two thumbs extend slowly upward.
Pointing to the paper, he breaks the language barrier
with a smile and two simple words:
Democracy: Good!

QRF²

Responsibility sucks.

Example A:

You've run the most consecutive missions of your unit,
but every streak must come to an end,
and if you know the lay of the land,
and the day's mission has maximum hazards,
and they need someone to run QRF,
that's the time the streak will cease to be.

It's a good thing,
being acknowledged
being given responsibility
but responsibility sucks.

Example B:

You're in the tower,
you don't have to be,
you're running QRF,
but just sitting and waiting isn't your thing.

So you're in the tower,
with a radio,
and binoculars,
and you're keeping tabs on the convoy,
and it's about five clicks out
when the tower shakes
accompanied by one of those discordant fulminations
you hate to be accustomed to.

So you grab the radio
and you check with the range

but they don't have anything going on
so you trade the radio for the binoculars
to find the smoke that's coming up
about five clicks out.

Switch frequencies.

Example C:

The convoy's been hit
or at least attacked,
no casualties to report…yet,
fire exchanged,
no need for QRF,
situation under control.
And you weren't there
to help your guys.

Responsibility sucks.

CARNIVALE, TARIN KOWT[3]

Macabre marionettes reel
the dance of the departed,

adorning the tower
or prostrating at its base,

a message left at
the epicenter of this vivid city.

Four roads seem to stretch forever
out from this dust-shrouded circle;

short mismatched buildings line
the intersecting avenues, crooked balconies

smiling down at children who
share streets with hens and strays.

It all revolves around a single point:
the emerald clock tower in circle's center.

This scene reminds me of Basseterre,
that vibrant Caribbean city,

bustling tropical metropolis
where one time I tried goat water.

In Basseterre at Carnivale they string
lights from the tower's top.

They snake out above rough pavement:
parallel celestial avenues.

But here, no lights are strung.

THE MOON'S STILL UP

When we first set out—it seems like days now,
though surely it's only hours—the moon hung heavy in the sky,
an insistent luminescence in green
while, through night vision, we picked our way
precisely through the desert night.

Now, as we stop before entering the pass ahead,
(a perfect place for ambush with its single narrow road,
high sloping walls, one way in and out)
the moon still hangs, resisting the desert sun's dominance.

I can't help but wonder why it's lingering,
what it's waiting to see—there's nothing
but a road that's barely discernible from the desert around it,
expanse interrupted violently by sharp mountains ahead of me,
and those behind, which somehow remind me of Scotland,
uneven, shadowed green trying to force its way out—
what in the landscape warrants staying in the sky today?

The seven trucks do their best to blend in,
men posed alert next to them, eyes begging
the mountains to reveal their secrets,
beads of sweat sneaking onto trigger fingers,
wondering what the moon is waiting to watch unfold.

4TH OF JULY

We get the day off.
Meaning no mission,
but it's never really off.

Maintenance on Humvees
precedes the day's festivities:
a meal a bit less greasy,
soccer with the Dutch,
a chance to call home.

The picnic's at my mother's house
and I can almost see them gathered
poolside, bare feet against the deck
that hostas try their best to breach,
plumes billowing from the grill
(I don't much like the sight of smoke now).

The whole family's there, even great-uncle Pat,
who asks with interest
if I've had the chance to
shoot any gooks?

His was a different time,
a different war.
It still persists within him,
shaping his perceptions of mine.

I laugh it off,
take in their telescopic voices
what could be one last time,
then head to the tower.
It's never really off, after all.

In the absence of fireworks
I fire off some flares
and wonder what this will look like
when my mind's had
sixty years to shape it.

TIGHTROPING TRUCKS

The soft expanse of Afghanistan's sky,
balloon announcing a baby boy,
stretches across—or out from—the spot
where a civilian car would sport an ornament—
a goddess, wildcat, surly mountain-dwelling creature—
but where I have only slightly beveled, sand-toned steel:
a sliver of tan, then blue. Nothing else in sight.

The 32.1 lbs of my vest and helmet, with an assist from gravity,
insists that I sit as far back in my seat as possible.
I was always mixed on roller coasters.
Loved the anticipation, the rush, the feel of leaving a part of me
237 ft. above and behind me.
Not the biggest fan of the feeling of the padded roll bar—
would it quite contain my scrawny frame?—
I hope this Humvee does as I force it to climb,
Doc Brown's words echoing in my head.

My gunner shouts down to me about obstacles to my front,
the Sgt. next to me lets me know just how close I am
to teetering—if such a heavy vehicle can teeter—over
the edge of the drop off to my right—only a few hundred meters
to the bottom—while to my left I stare nearly straight down
at sand, rock, obstinate tufts of grass that lead only slightly
more gently to a different bottom.
My knuckles seem tensed to pounce on some unseen prey,
knowing the lives of these two men—
art school, the girl he wants to marry for my gunner,
the Sergeant's wife, kids, new house he bought on leave—
rest entirely in my hands' ability
to keep the wheel at just the right degree while driving blind.

HEADLIGHTS

Like fireflies they swarm,
a luminescent dance in
the otherwise black of
the late desert night.

Perched in the hills,
refusing to allow sleep's
duplicitous tendrils to
envelop me, I watch

as the lightning bugs'
choreography reveals
a convergence. From
east and west and north

they float down mountains,
drawn to the point that
sits below my own. This
ballet, at first so tranquil and

inviting, foreshadows
its brutal final act.

SKA IN THE WADI

Constant vigilance.

That's what's needed to survive here.
(I know this because they told us before we even came.)

But sanity is important too (or so I assume),
so I made some minor modifications to the Humvee I drive each day
(minor because, let's face it, between a couple radios, navigation computer,
my armor, my rifle, extra ammo, water, etc. there's not much spare room).

One miniature, flat speaker.
One piece of Velcro, 1" X 3".
One iPod determined to survive the dust.

It's barely audible,
but just enough to keep me upbeat and alert.

Rolling through villages, threats around every corner,
the Bosstones' *wahd* guitars keep me amped.

Zoot Suit Riot's heavy drums make my heart rate seem less drastic.

Setzer's horns swing me up and out of riverbeds.

Yeah, L-T, that is the *Bumblebee Tuna Song*.

CHESS AT THE GATE

He plays the way his beard would indicate:
swift, but calculated
speed allowed by years of whitening experience.
There's no trace of grey.

Calm, and precise
in placing his fingertips atop each piece
just prior to its gentle relocation.

He speaks little, this venerable translator,
choosing his words carefully when he must
so I am not surprised when he slides his knight into place,
quietly declares check mate, and sits back to indicate game's end.

There is the usual silence that follows his victory:
I replay his moves and mine in an attempt to improve my own game,
until it is broken by his sigh, the type usually reserved for my own defeat.
He strives for casual as his chosen words inform me that his son
is being held by Taliban, taken because he followed in his father's footsteps,
quiet desert chess master, ally to the enemy.

III

LINES COMPOSED A FEW MILES ABOVE KANDAHAR

On the eight day move from Shit Fob[4] A to Shit Fob B, we make a brief stop in Kandahar, booming metropolis of RC South, brief—yet so long with the civilized we all begin to fidget—just long enough to test out of a college course—Freshman Comp—though the proctor, on learning I was Infantry, made gallant attempts at dissuasion. I would later learn I aced it. Upon arrival, one of the first things I hear is of the boardwalk: recently mortared… again. Attention tends to draw itself to the final piece, the "yet again", the implication of iteracy, of ingemination. Of recurrence, repetition, and redundancy—a touch of tedium—insipid entry in the lookout's log. My mind wanders from finish to start as it begins to process this piece of news, the hook—wait—boardwalk. Yes. Here, somewhere between Shit Fob A and Shit Fob B, there lies a boardwalk. Must be meant ironically (if only that proctor could see me now), as we would sometimes name places back at and around Shit Fob A. I must get a look. I do. It is. Not ironic, I mean, but full-fledged boardwalk, the cream filling of this, our kind hostess. Coffee shop: Mark-19[5] and a Boston Cream? Burger joint, American pizza place—and whytheHell not? American pizza in Afghanistan: just the same as the Chicago Pizzeria in Kenmore Square—some things in life transplant themselves. It's no Atlantic City, true, but boardwalk just the same. I am in awe. Not that Shit Fob A was really all that bad: we had cement structures, a building with running water (even if the piss-tubes were closer). The Dutch would always have warm bread, and I knew of Van Nistelrooy, from ManU to Madrid, even knew of Eindhoven—my ticket to warm rolls. I heard about a Fob that once served the Soviet rich—a resort, now resorted, redrawn to suit these new inhabitants. Some have only tents. It's tents we're headed for—Shit Fob B more shit than A. But here: a promenade: shop-lined like the Riviera. Basketball courts—day 2: we beat the Canadians at street hockey (five desert months released on an orange ball)—and a promenade, the type of place where cleanliness of uniforms is questioned, where salutes are actually expected (not seen as sniper's signifier), where for two brief days (and two too long) we live in luxury. Where literacy and iteracy and infantry can coexist. Where sand beneath boardwalks doesn't hint of salt. A fuckin' boardwalk.

WHEN FLYING IN HELICOPTERS AT NIGHT

It doesn't matter how much sleep you haven't gotten,
your adrenaline won't let you sleep on the flight.

The "seats" are uncomfortable: acutely angled, steel and webbing pews,
but at least you're not the guy hanging out the back with a machine gun.

The thing's fuckin' loud (this will also keep you from sleeping),
there's no sense talking, but if you sing to calm your nerves, no one will hear you.

The pilot's going to hug the ridgeline to keep a low profile,
when you close your eyes to counter nausea, replay the mission plan in your head.

You're getting dropped in at night because it's dangerous,
don't expect to leave before the sun goes down.

When the rotors are lost in something louder and the back fills with smoke,
grip your weapon, assess the situation: count the guys next to and across from you,

check and make sure there's still a guy hanging out the back,
don't bother trying to slow down your heart rate (your adrenaline won't let you),

and when you realize he hugged the ridgeline a little too close,
breathe, then go ahead and curse the pilot. No one will hear you.

RADIO

The box crackles to life.

There is no pulse-quickening beat,
no revolutionary lyric.

There is no jazz
smoothly flowing through frequencies;
no easy-listening host whose sultry
voice says it's time to take it slow…

There is no slow.

There is no millionaire
multi-platinum rapper
preaching the 'hard life'.

There is no cigar-smoking suit
telling the nation what to think,
how to act,
talking of policies and distant realities.

There is no distant.

A story emerges from the static:

bullets fly through airwaves.

Man down—men down.

Men not getting up.

We listen to horrors kilometers away.

The mountains between us
may as well be continents.

White noise:
we wait.

VIGIL

His eyes flash recognition.

This man who sits in shadowed corner,
ears tuned to the metal box at his side,
eyes now fixed on a point invisible to all but him;

they strain to find some truth in mountains.
Mine cannot stray from this man who sits and
waits, and listens, and maintains his distant gaze.

What must he think as he sends his signal
out toward God, to receive only
Death on frequency's return?

I do not ask his name, but rely instead on
the tape across his chest, opposite his heart:
that shoulder bears the flag he fights for.

This same flag must adorn some distant,
slumping shoulder. This same fight lost
across the mountains, carried to him
through frequencies, through unanswered
prayers that cross foreign lips, through
this box that keeps his mourning company,

this box that keeps me riveted. I do not know
him beyond what his uniform speaks. I do not
know the names the radio emits across this tiny
plot of land we find ourselves defending,
but in my distance, in the silence we both keep,
I join the box, and keep his mourning company.

I WANT TO PAINT THE SUNRISE

But I've never been skilled with brush.

I want to paint the softness of this sunrise I'm seeing.
If for no other reason than it seems surreal. Or too real.

To have canvas on easel
Palette and brush

and in strokes panoramic like the hills
that hide the mountains
the sun sneaks out of,
capture this moment in visual aubade
knowing I've made it through another night alone—alive—
watching, , listening, waiting for the landscape to reappear,
knowing there's only a couple more such nights ahead of me,
hoping I make it through those—alive—and home.

To turn this wooden platform
from east tower to studio.

To have canvas on easel
palette and brush

machine gun
ammo belts
binoculars
grenades
flares
sandbags
barb wire frame

I want to paint the sunrise.

TOURS

It started with a fall in the spring. I couldn't have known that going off the back of a 5-ton truck (a little more than a six-foot fall) in the so-called safe way the Army trained me in could lead to a world tour. Not that alone, but having my leg ripped apart in the process, not externally so, but on the inside, as all the soft stuff in the knee and the ankle tore, and the knee cap took a bit of a wee wander, and the shin cracked in four different places, just not enough to break it, and the hip went where it's not quite supposed to. This the result of my right boot's toe getting caught in a mounting stirrup that should've been down, gravity and full combat gear bringing my body to the ground in a head first twist while my foot stayed on the truck bed.

That's what led to my tour. The tour that ended the Tour.

I. BAGRAM

We stop at Bagram, the last holdover on the move from Shit FOB A to Shit FOB B. Another one of those bases where a front-liner's sensibility can't help but question. This one even has a Starbucks, a movie theatre, and chaos outside the gate that rivals a Mexico City street market. The drive into Little America takes us past burned out cars, bullet-riddled mud walls and huts with roofs of corrugated tin—maybe it was aluminum—just an hour before that day's first explosions. This is where it starts.

We're here, in the closest thing to civilization we've had, and Beebs wants me to see the ortho while one's available. I'm fortunate to have such a strong platoon sergeant. Never questioned him. Never had to. Now I do. Insist I can't go see the surgeon. He'll send me out of here. I've made it this far, four months since injury. I am the epitome of the (unofficial) infantry code: suck it up and drive on. Probably sounds better in Latin. My respectful disagreement doesn't sway him. I make my way to the hospital, trying not to let my knee buckle within his eyeshot.

Some things are consistent. I mean, ever been to Chinatown, or Little Italy, and most of it's about as unauthentic as you could think, but some things are just right? I wait. And wait. And wait. This doctor's visit feels like home. He checks out the leg, asks all the questions. I could have written the script. I'm typically at a 4-6 (that's the face that looks more constipated than anything). When aggravated an 8 or 9 (the face that looks like it's just a face because some sort of wildcat got the rest of him). More buckles than a pirate get-up. Shakes? You bet. One word: Medevac. He wants me out of the shit, off to Germany. Shit. Hate to say "Itoldyouso."

II. MEDEVAC

It's a C-130. They put us in the big hollow belly, sitting in cargo seats (I never want to hear someone complain about coach again). These are basically netting strung between metal bars. Just wide enough to fit a size 2. But we're the lucky ones. Some make the flight on a rack of stretchers, stacked like baker's sheets in the center of the hold. We're the lucky ones. We know that others make the journey with us: on the cargo list. Not on stretchers. Not in chairs. My fellow passengers are all in various states of disarray. I look fine. If it weren't for the massive tag on my bag—manila with a blatant red cross—I may have been part of the crew. Except for the shade of my uniform. Our uniforms are always more stained and faded. Laundry was not a priority back on Shit FOB A. It won't be at Shit FOB B.

It's amazing that such a massive hunk of metal can make it into the air. A miracle it stays there. But damn is it slow. I can't keep my knee in one position for very long. Have to unstrap myself, stretch it. Put weight on. Take weight off. I guess this is why I'm here. Here among the hidden. These are the ones the papers don't mention. They only want to number the dead.

Sleep comes in fits. My neck feels worse than my knee. The noise. The noise. The noise. It's noisy. And cold. These beasts are shells. No insulation. Maybe a little. Not much. It's cold. And noisy. We land.

III. KUWAIT

The plane's so slow, so big, so heavy. It's slow. We can't make it all the way from Afghanistan to Germany. Googlemaps can't even figure out how far it is. More than 3000 miles. It's far. The plane's slow. We stop in Kuwait. Back into the desert heat. Then they fuck up. Not too bad, I guess. I mean, they didn't cut open the wrong leg. But they kept me in Kuwait. My tag says Germany. I'm lost luggage. They keep me in Kuwait. It's interesting. They don't have what they need on base, so I get to go into the city. I have to buy jeans, shoes, polos. Civvies. Here I dress like what I am not. But what I'm on my way to being. The image of what I used to be.

Kuwait City. It sits on the Persian Gulf, a sapphire in the sands, sun dancing off innumerable facets. It's the first real water I've seen all year. Home again. Water means home to me. It's why I got the tattoo the week before I left. So I'd always have home with me. The Keys. The Sound. The West Branch. They go where I go now. But now the Persian Gulf.

The drive up to this point was strange. Eerie is maybe a better word. Uncanny? Twilight-Zoney. Zone-ish? We're driving through the desert, just like I've been doing for the past few months. The people are dressed in their traditional garb, just like I've seen the past few months. But they're driving Benzes. Audis. Not Hiluxes. And we're just driving. No tactical stops. No comms. No caution. I'm uncomfortable in the back of the van, watching cars approach us from the rear, watching them pass. This is unnatural. Totally normal at home. But unnatural for me now. Here. Just because I think of home, just because I'm reminded of it, doesn't mean I'm there. I close my eyes.

The city is a hybrid. East meets West in purest form. Sand meets Starbucks. Hajis meet Hardee's. Uncanny again. Maybe even confusing. We get to the hospital. Automatic doors. Weird again. The waiting room is pleasant. Tea is served. Soap operas are on the television. A movie from a few years before I was born. The staff is courteous. Beyond that—they are kind. Sincere. The MRI is something else. The tube has never bothered me. The holding still. Not even the noise. They give you headphones, pump in music. But here, this is the problem for me. It's Kuwaiti covers of Bolton. Uncanny. No, unbearable. Like Shit FOB A, and all that happened there, I survive. I guess in light of it all, the Bolton covers are nothing. I shouldn't have been so harsh. I've been through worse.

Many more have been through worse than me. Some were on the cargo list...

MRIs are done, we go back to base. This is no FOB. Not even a Little America. This is nice. Prime. The comfort is uncomfortable. An Olympic size pool. A shopping center. Two shopping centers. Even a Taco Bell. But the fake-meat-filling doesn't taste quite right. Not even hot sauce can hide the fact that this isn't home. It's a hastily contrived reproduction. Thrown together. Perfect from afar. Missing the finer points. Results are back in a few days. Inconclusive. They send me back.

IV. BAGRAM (AGAIN)

The flight back is the same. The plane is slow. There isn't much insulation. It's cold. There's noise. The plane is slow. I'm finally back where I feel I belong. Well, not quite. This is Little America. I belong out at Shit FOB B. I miss Shit FOB A. I miss my guys. My rifle.

I'm off the plane, into the medical building. Waiting. Waiting. Waiting. I used to wait tables. Now I wait for doctors. They don't know why I'm there. I'm supposed to be in Germany. I inform them of a place called Kuwait (*It's really quite lovely*). They aren't amused. I wasn't supposed to be there. I was supposed to be in Germany. I'm going on the next flight out.

V. GERMANY

Another flight to Kuwait. This time they don't keep me there. I'm glad about that. Kuwait was different. It was pleasant. Just not for me. I meet new people. I don't remember their names. I don't forget them. I just don't remember (I think there's a difference). This is where my tag said I was supposed to be all along, and here I am. Germany is entirely different. A veritable Wonderland, horrors and joys alike. Often I find that they're the same. There is no sand. The sun is bashful. Maybe embarrassed: it cries after hiding. It's very different, but much of the same. Doctors. Waiting. Tests, MRIs, X-Rays, shopping centers. I have to buy more clothes. I brought some civvies with me when I deployed. Jeans, my favorite shorts, board shorts, some tees, a hoodie. But they're all in a footlocker in a connex in Afghanistan somewhere between Shit FOB A and Shit FOB B. Maybe they've arrived by now. Maybe they've been blown up. That seems more likely. So I go shopping. An American soldier in Germany, I buy an English-tailored suit. I embody the cooperative spirit of NATO. The hospital is white. Institutional. Sterile. Not the makeshift field med station of Shit FOB A. Not the haphazard buildings of Bagram. No colors like in Kuwait. White.

They tell me I'll be here awhile. Set me up in a small housing base away from the hospital and the main base, the one with the shopping mall. I have a room, some roommates. We're all there for different reasons. Reasons I don't remember. Except for one. She's not a roommate because she's a she (the Army isn't big on co-ed). We meet in a lounge, waiting to get passes to get off the base and into town. Not that the base is boring. Much nicer than Shit FOB A. Behind the residence hall there's a bar. German wheat beer. Hefewiezen and Weissbier. I'm a one-and-done. I guess six months in the desert takes away your tolerance. There are slots in the back. I win a couple hundred bucks. Shoes to match my suit. Maybe Italian.

So the base isn't bad. But I've been in the sandbox for six months. I can see trees over the fence now. Hills that roll instead of erupting. So I make an acquaintance waiting for permission to hit the town. To see old churches, drink more Weissbier, catch some soccer. Churches, no cathedrals: like I used to see on vacation. We explore. She's kind. Fun. And a she. A break from the sand, a break from the sun, a break from the dryness, a break from testosterone. Her break from the stress. She cracked. Something about wanting to roll a grenade into her commander's tent. I mean don't we all want to do that at some point? But I guess we don't all verbalize it. So she got a trip to Germany. Nice prize for saying what we all think.

Kleber. Kaiserslautern. I ride a fish. There are fish all over Kaiserslautern, but I only ride one of them: part of an elaborate fountain depicting pieces of the city's rich lore. There's an owl, with glasses. A pair of loving donkeys. A lord and lady: headless so we can "wear" them. And a fish, which we ride. And churches. Cathedrals. A museum. And Weissbier. And Irish beer. I like it here.

The next day my knee gives out.

Maybe I walked too much. It was a long uphill to the *stadio*. I'm heading downstairs on the way to breakfast when it decides to give out. I fall. I brace myself. I fracture my wrist. Just a little. But enough. It's ok though. I'm going to the hospital later anyway. I go. I wait. I see a doctor. They want me to leave Germany. To go what they call "stateside", what I call home. Called home. But it's not where I should be. Perspective changes definitions, and they can't send me without consent from my commander. Shit FOB B is isolated; communication is not easy. I have to go back. This is a victory for me. I am broken, but returning to where I belong. Goodbye rain. Goodbye hills. Goodbye rain falling onto the hills.

VI. BAGRAM (AGAIN AGAIN)

Another flight. Slow. Cold. Noisy. Slow. They almost fucked up again. See, Bagram sounds a bit like Balad (I guess). So they almost put me on a plane there. Imagine that. From Afghanistan to Kuwait and back again, then

Germany and onto Iraq! I catch it. They just catch my bag. Back to Bagram. More waiting. Most of my guys have long since headed out. Up to Shit FOB B. Some are back for supplies though. I join them. It's a long drive. Slow. Noisy. Hot. A new part of the country though. Past lakes that used to be stories higher, the toll of too many arid days marked by lines on the cliffs that now watch over them. The cliffs that used to be below. Things change. My wrist is well enough for me to have my rifle back. I need it taped and wrapped though. The drive is long. Slow. Painful. Hot. I can't keep my knee in one position too long. Up-armoreds aren't known for their legroom. It could be worse. I could be cargo. The scenery is harsh. Astoundingly beautiful. I have that. And I am back with those whose names I know. Whose names I still remember.

VII. KALA GUSH (SHIT FOB B)

A drastic shift from the desert expanse that somehow I grew used to, this makeshift base they want us to call home. Tents and connex boxes, a trailer for showers. HESCOs and sandbags connecting towers, the only operations I get to know. No more missions, no more patrols. The knee just can't handle it. I'm a hazard. Not the asset I used to be. Useless. A Disney princess confined to my tower, no longer the dashing rescuer. I fought to get back to this, but I can no longer fight the fight they need me to. A hazard. So they arrange a chopper to get me back to Bagram, to get me back to Bragg, to fix my knee, so that maybe I won't always be so useless. It will take two weeks for transport to come for me. Two weeks of towers. Two weeks of trailer showers. Two weeks of knowing that the men around me will have to stay among these mountains while I go over them. To safety. To certainty. To not knowing who leads each mission. Not knowing who will come back. Just knowing I can do nothing to ensure they all do…

VIII. FLIGHTS

It's a real plane. Not slow. Not noisy. Not cold. No cargo nets. I won't complain about coach. And I don't. But before we push off, an officer comes back from first class. There's one seat open (*What grunt wishes to sit among the great?*). Many raise their hands. My wrist is wrapped. They notice. I can't keep my knee in one position too long. First class has more leg room—the leather seats are not up-armored. I move. There are movies playing throughout the flight. I let them form the backdrop for my thoughts. The soundtrack for my fading waking. The flight is long. Even though this plane is not slow.

There is a greater distance that must be covered here.

RAINING IN GERMANY

A sea of black spreads out around me as the first drops fall.
One by one, umbrellas open, shielding passersby on their journeys.
The rain beats, beads, rolls along and off their streamlined domes.

My hands remain free, palms upturned.

I look to the sky and let the rain run over me
eyes closed, my journey unfolding in my mind.
My parched skin soaks up each drop
like those countless crimson floods are taken in
by the arid sands I've left behind.

It has been too long since rain has brushed this body.
I will not hide from it.
I will embrace it.

It's raining in Germany
and I am halfway home.

IV

HARTSFIELD

Cane in hand, I disembark,
reentering the world I used to know.

This newly launched assault—
fast-food fries, PAs, central air, beeping trolleys,
spliced with applause, handshakes, and strangers' thanks—
stark contrast to silent desert nights.

Validation.

Pride—in what I've done.
Tears—for where I am. And what I've left behind.

I have found the answer.

It is home.

SHORTLY THEREAFTER

I crash.

It is not the burning rubber and twisted metal
of a car careening into a guardrail, the wheel cut
to avoid some common piece of Turnpike trash.

It is not the sound of the lamp hitting the floor,
knocked from the table as I leaped out of bed,
jolted awake by the dumpster hitting the ground.

It is not the door, shut so hard it swings back open
as she leaves. *This isn't what we wanted* still ringing
in my ears, as the cat looks on inquisitively.

It is the loss of the high of home.
The sudden realization of nothing.

GEAR SHIFT

1

I've heard
so much
about this
straw I
seek but
cannot find
the point
to break.

2

Shackled and
suffocating,
I need a free fall.

3

Bottles beckon.
Ounce by ounce I drown.

4

I'm sick of all this idealistic
cheap   romantic,
hypocritical idolatry.
Craving that cold, harsh
unforgiving reality,
that place with no room
for shades of grey,
that blanket of achromatic ash.

5

As the needle creeps
toward ninety
my eyes begin
to glaze,
blurring the speedometer's
blue and red.

My mind needs only seconds
for the image to unfold:
more twisted metal,
maybe flames.
Or maybe I just coast,
spin, emerge unscathed.
I can't decide.

I just want to cut
the wheel.
Close
my eyes.
Throw
myself
into the unwilling
Arms—of Allah.

BOTTLE OPENER

Shades drawn, I sit on the floor and pry
my honor's edge under corrugated rim: first
of six. Release cutting illusion of silence
drone of the muted box, unseen
where I contemplate and combat
the spin-out since coming home.

I wanted nothing more than home,
those I'd missed, but others pried
into events of seven months in combat.
I was bombarded with inquiries first,
before I could even process what I'd seen.
I greet them with a distant stare and silence.

In Uruzgan, in rare moments of silence
and solitude I would cling desperately to home:
New England's shell strewn shores, not children's blood seen
spilled on sand, a violent new day-by-day to pry
me from my dreams. Mission first.
Constant alert, plan, execute: the rhythm of combat.

MOS 11B: Infantryman. Front line combat,
my weapon's frequent bursts will lead to silence
ringing. I am not the first
to earn this badge, to risk home
to protect abstractions. It's not about fighting those who try to pry
Freedom or Democracy away from a place they've never seen;

it's protecting those few who share what you have seen,
brothers in arms, strangers made inseparable through combat
until death, or injury, or pride, or peace begin to pry
you apart. I am a recluse, an uninvited vow of silence
and isolation, an early, guilt-ridden return home.
The injury I tried to push through. Med-Evac. Not the first

injured to leave my platoon, and even though at first
I fought to stay, when the knee began to give, when doctors had seen
the damage, the incapacitation, the risk I posed, I was bound for home.
Forced to leave the violent province, newfound brothers, life of combat,
return to this life that lacks adrenal kicks, my head hung in the silence
Of guilt, pain, personal defeat, and the slow slipping away of pride.

Now I assault this six-pack, try to pry myself away from all I've seen,
from the silence of being caught between those I left in combat,
and the unknowing faces of home that once were first to know me.

BOTTLE OF SUNSHINE

They were yellow.

                      Mocking.

12 1/2 milligrams of sunshine. Up the dose for rainbows.

I hated them.

                      Crave them.

Cold turkey's no way to go. Supposed to wean.
But weaning takes time I didn't think I had.

Banished that bottle to the bottom drawer.
With the sleepers. And the pain killers.

                      And the pain.

I couldn't think of consequences I didn't know.
Just had to pass the piss test.
Had to enlist.

                      Do something.

And I did.
I pissed.
I passed.
And they put me on a plane.

                      Pain multiplies in darkness.

Across the Atlantic.
Over the Hindu Kush.
Into the desert.

                      And back.

I thought I could handle the return.
Had to.
Had to just be a twenty-something.
Had to redefine normal. Again.

                      Ignore the spirals.

Classes. Work. Classes. Work.
Work. To forget. Keep the hands moving.
Keep the legs moving.
Even if it hurts with each right stride.
Through the pops.
Shelve the pain.

                                              Send it back to breed in darkness.

But what's buried will rise.

And now I miss the 12.5.

CIGARETTES

French for 'small cigar',
ignite and let smolder,
like memories.

Hemingway and Miro:
Paris' smoke-screened glamour
in grainy black and white.

On high risk missions,
light to cut tension
increase alertness.

Post firefight, one slow
long drag will ease the
stress, unleash the mind.

On a cool night's watch,
beneath the cover of a cup,
inhale to stay awake.

But when all is done,
and little said,
and battles are behind us,

we smoke to help
our hands forget
the weight of rifles.

MIGRATORY

A living monument to Foucault,
I hang suspended as
the world moves around me.
A single character paused
while the film plays on.

I reenter the world a year too late:
the bird that missed migration.

My uniform lies at the back of my closet
untouched,
unneeded.

My camouflage has changed.

THE SECOND STORY WINDOW
DOESN'T SEEM SO HIGH

Or maybe it does.

I find it hard to know just what I think these days. I cannot trust the thoughts I think I think—I think.

In war I thought it all was so uncertain, but uncertainty was guaranteed. But here, college, and of all places freshmen Psych class, where certainty should be ensured by class lists and start times, I'm uncertain once more. And this window doesn't seem so high.

I wouldn't think of jumping (though clearly I just did). And if I can't trust the thoughts I think I think should I put faith in the unthinkable?

Other students are looking out the window too. This window with a perfect view of approach routes, of the roof of the buildings across the street, of the main intersection. The seventeen cars that have passed. The three that have done so twice. Are the others noticing these things too? Are they aware how high it is? Or isn't?

My peers (though it somehow seems unfit to use that word—I never complain about the weight of my backpack), they daydream. They gaze, detached, out the window because out there is not in here and in here there is a woman talking, droning, about drinking. Alcohol.

I drink alcohol. Beer mostly, but never the cheap stuff. I was cursed with a palate. Sometimes wine. This palate is developing. But that's out there. And out there is not in here. I cannot drink in here because in here is school and out there is not, though I learn (and maybe more). And in here, here being school, there is a woman talking about alcohol.

Some guys (boys?) have stopped looking out there and begun to pay attention to this woman. She has asked who in here drinks alcohol out there. These fellows think they're cool. I can tell because they nudge and do the "bro-nod." Chuckles. I indicate, more reverently, that I can be counted in this category.

She moves in.

Questioning, frowning. Why? How? Fake ID? I must be wrong. This is a class for freshmen. This is why she is here. To talk to first years about their first years and the dangers we've been warned of since 7th grade.

But the dangers I've faced did not come from college bars, from darkened street corners. The four years that separate me from those wedged into desks around me carried me to places they only see in books, on TV. No streets for corners, no college for bars. Just violence from an unknown enemy. That was always certain.

So now I sit, and think the thoughts I think or dare not to, and while those around me dream, I can't help but notice that this window doesn't seem so high.

KILL COUNT

It's the first thing they ask.
Any time.
Every time.
Everytime.

No "yes/no" frame,
only assumed negation
the answer must be numbers,
not just a word,
laden with implication.

I speak to them of sensitivity,
of difficulties of such situations,
that I am willing to share my story,
but others may react much differently,
I think the answer: zero. None.
No, if only I had the framework.

And I think the answer, that zero, that non-
number, and I think it with
Relief?
Regret?
Shame?
More shame for my response?

And I explain to them about the importance
of protection, that my focus lies on lives protected,
not taken. Numbers:
the funerals attended,
flags seen draped, then folded.

Sorrow.
Relief.
Regret.

I was the kid who would bring the spiders back outside,
not introduce them to the back of my favorite book.
That would yield regret. The funerals, sorrow.

But here I had a job unfinished,
and maybe curiosity: could I have done it,
if faced with such necessity? I'd like to think I would,
I could to save the lives of those around me,
like some I served with were forced to do.

Relief.
Release.
Relief.

I'M REMINDED MORE IN WINTER

When the cold works its way into scar tissue
once again informing me that I am not the same
as those around me, not a "typical" 25-year-old,
that the scars are not from some football injury
not a torn MCL on the hardwood like so many assume.

I'm reminded more in winter of what it is I cannot do:
it's not that I'm not out running—
I never liked running in the cold—
it's when the snow starts to melt,
and race season is just around the corner,
and I know that I won't be on the road.

I'm reminded more in winter
not of what I've been through,
(New England's freeze never evokes
Uruzgan's summer blazes)
but of what it was I missed:
those missions in the mountains,
through the snow,
through countless attacks I couldn't defend,
through poor command decisions,
and the separation from loved ones
articulated by spotty comms.

I'm reminded more in winter
when the stiffness and the stabbing pain
keep me from the sleep my nightmares need to thrive.

MONUMENTS

We are not statues
standing among the trees,
a tribute to what has passed.

We are not statues,
though our faces are stone,
chiseled by time, shaped by history
that we are now part of,
as it is part of us.

We are living monuments,
stoic in the shadows
as the world around us moves.

SPECIAL THANKS

There are so many people who made this book possible. First I have to thank all of the guys of 3rd Platoon, C Co. 1-102, the TK/KG PRT, and 7th Group for getting me home alive. Obviously without you guys there would be no book. Michael White, for taking a shot at letting a vet attempting to write into his MFA program; Elizabeth Hastings for keeping me on schedule; Bill Patrick, Baron Wormser, Kim Bridgford, and Sarah Manguso for leading workshops and master classes, and helping me find my voice and delve into my content; all of the FUMFAers who workshopped my pieces (and especially thanks to those who were in my workshop the week after my leg reconstruction…that could not have been easy!); and to Elizabeth Kirschner, under whose watchful eye this manuscript came together. To Dave Cappella, and Aimee Pozorski, who encouraged me to pursue writing and an MFA in the first place. Abby, without your support and encouragement, and tolerance for my stereotypically 'poetic' moments, I'm not sure I would have pulled this off. Becca, thanks for being there through the early processes, and for getting me the shoes that would become my signature and Twitter handle. Very special thanks to Chris and Neil, who bought many rounds when I decided to quit my job and be a writer; next one's on me. To Erin Curtis for reading countless early drafts and being my photographer at lectures; Chelsee for reviewing drafts (still), giving invaluable insights, and shedding tears of affirmation; Amanda Lister (and her 09-10 freshmen honors class) for giving me my first workshop opportunity; the Goldfarb Foundation for funding workshop development, Liz Devine, Carol Blejwas, and the students and administration of Hall High School for welcoming me with open arms and allowing me to share my passions with you. Jilissa Hope Milner, Kindra McDonald, Charlotte Gullick, Chris Leche, and Kelly Singleton-Dalton, working with you on creating a better world for those impacted by war has been and will continue to be an honor and pleasure. And to my baristas at the Bishop's Corner and Newton Plaza Starbucks who kept me caffeinated through the writing and submission processes, thank you. To my late grandfather, Raymond H. Densmore, whose final gift to me was the realization that poetry can heal. To my mother and Matt, who bought me my first notebook way back when, and gave encouragement, even when I decided to pursue (gasp!) an advanced degree in creative writing. Brenden and Liz, for that familial support and a couch to crash on when I needed an escape to rediscover my voice; Lauren for picking me up when the rejections rolled in and sharing in my life, joy, and advocacy—your passion keeps me going on the days when I can't quite find the spark. Those of you who know me and should also be thanked here will know that if your name does not appear, that's just me being my scatter-brained self. Finally, to reiterate the dedication, my deepest gratitude to Erica Cuni, who helped me find my voice and understand my experiences through writing about them. I hope that my voice can serve as proxy to those vets who are still seeking their own, and that through my writing and their own, our veterans can gain an understanding which they can then pass on to those who have not been through it.

—CDH

NOTES

"Mister Shingles," page 19
> [1]CR: Casualty Radius—The area from the point of detonation in which at least 50% of exposed personnel sustain injuries or death.

"QRF," page 34
> [2]Quick Reaction Force: any force that is poised to respond on very short notice, typically less than fifteen minutes.

"Carnival, Tarin Kowt," page 36
> [3]The small capital of Uruzgan Province, Afghanistan

"Lines Composed a Few Miles Above Kandahar," page 47
> [4]Fob: Forward Operating Base
> [5]MK-19: Belt-fed automatic 40 mm grenade launcher